LANDSCAPE WITH LIGHT

ALSO BY JON THOMPSON

POETRY
The Book of the Floating World

ESSAYS
Fiction, Crime and Empire
After Paradise: Essays on the Fate of American Writing

JON THOMPSON

LANDSCAPE WITH LIGHT

SHEARSMAN BOOKS

First published in the United Kingdom in 2014 by
Shearsman Books
50 Westons Hill Drive
Emersons Green
BRISTOL BS16 7DF

Shearsman Books Ltd Registered Office
30–31 St. James Place, Mangotsfield, Bristol BS16 9JB
(this address not for correspondence)

www.shearsman.com

ISBN 978-1-84861-349-2

Contents

To my mother, Claire Thompson
To my sisters, Sara, Elizabeth & Megan
To my wife, Suzanne
And to my daughters, Zoe & Sofie

What I am interested in now is the landscape. Pictures without people. I wouldn't be surprised if eventually there are no people in my pictures. It is so emotional.
– Annie Leibovitz

Letter to Jim Jarmusch

(Broken Flowers)

What they'll know of us in future years: the large interiors of our suburban homes were designed by others & lacking in the slightest trace of individual taste. Were cavernous & costly & sterile, mausoleums to the fashion of the moment. Lives were lived in them, but not so they'd disturb the silk cushions on the crushed velvet settees. The air in them was still & muted & old, as if marked by a recent death. Outside, away from the cul-de-sacs, the highways would buzz with traffic, particularly during the morning rush hour & the tired evening commute. Whizzing along, motion is a green forest bordering the sharp bends in the road. To fly, they'd take themselves to airports, with even more cavernous spaces and roofs that were wavy with no feeling in them, but were said to imitate the topography of the land. When not running panicked, people would saunter in them, tourists of their own lives. Indifference & consumption like muzak, everywhere. Once in the air, mall-life was brought to them, tranquilized at 25,000 feet with sunlight scintillating off polished airplane wings. Night was chain hotels with fake everything. Looking through a hotel window at a mass-produced, urban morning, you could see the way highways would wind in and out of gas stations and signage, like some long, slowly-dying hope. But thanks for giving us another Lolita, concupiscent in the buff, hot for her Humbert Humbert. And for all the road-trip emotions, the different shadings of feeling as the car nosed through the countryside (or was it the past?), under tree-limbs dappled with sunlight or into stricken suburban streets. Thanks for showing the poignancy of airport parking-lots. Poignancy of missing people; arrivals; departures.

Snow As Versions of Different Things
(*Fargo*)

DESIRE

In the flat uninhabited spaces, snow falls from an empty sky. Here and there, the bare branches of an oak are black against the steadily-falling flakes. When the air is thick with them, it's not white, exactly, but a glowing bluish-white, shading to grey as evening comes on, darkness in tow. Snow accumulates like loneliness, one snowfall covering the last one, layering into snowdrifts that become the landscape.

NAÏVETÉ

The landscape is cruel in its monotony, in its lethality. Cleverness here can lead to intolerable frustration. Better to cultivate a good-humored disposition to living in the here-and-now, becoming a connoisseur of the quotidian. Naïveté may be thought of as a form of regional loyalty, in which a seemingly-naive individual elects to embrace a culture lacking in prestige. It's possible that a naïf may be best suited to interpreting signs; it's possible that those regarded as naïve may evidence genius.

SILENCE

Genius of the winter sun is that it makes the cold white expanses theatrical. Every sound happens between silences; silence is the default condition of the land. Sudden noises, mechanical noises, appear to violate something like a primeval natural compact. For many, the long silences punctuated by soughing winds, are unendurable, a Nordic torment that goes with the long darkness, the deep cold. In a land defined by long silences, there are no successful lies.

Death

Lies, unworthy of the earth, lie buried in the snow, intact until snowmelt. The fields, the trees, the sky, the heart-clenching cold – even the ice sheeting the highway blacktop – exist as a reminder of the imminence of death: domain of the high, shiny, blue-black, earth-scanning things. Death makes us statuary. Though few seek it, everyone finds the white gift of oblivion. Everyone forced to forge new paths of exile through an unknown land.

A Panic That Dares Not Speak Its Own Name
(*Somewhere*)

Sapphire-blue pools & palm trees;
stillness of the strictly pacifico.

Luxury like a pill-whitened
loneliness.

Freeways that spaghetti the city
are one way

of easing it.
Watching the low smooth mountains

take the afternoon light
is another.

Fragment of an Unpublished Memoir
by a Cinematographer's Assistant
(*No Country For Old Men*)

"…riches of the world receding.
The desert was a landscape of mutability in a world of
immutability: I remember aimless cloud-shadows, slow-
dragging across the desert floor; high peaks of mountains
further off; light leaking from uninhabited heights. I
remember expanses dotted with mesquite & creosote,
wind rustling through them, the dry lilt of a back-country
song. Everything there & half erased. Mostly, I remember
the wide-open emptiness, with the yellow dividing
lines going through it. And a phrase from somewhere –
terrible lie– 'Suffering is so beautiful & sad…'"

Blue Is the Color of a Knowledge
That's Continually Unfolding
(25th Hour)

Where to put the regret,
the loss? Night
falls on the world's
most famous skyline,
Manhattan lit up –
splendid excess –
laid out behind Brooklyn
Bridge's necklaced
elegance. Blackness,
the invisible beauty.
You want
restitution. In place of
it, blue beams,
"the twin towers of
light," ascend upward,
astrally, piercing
the darkness. So much
distance to defy.
What was, invisible.
Absence most
visible.

You Think It's You, But It's Really Not
(*Training Day*)

The endless need to begin again. A white sun
ascends a desert sky. Perfect sheen
of brightness on sun-drenched streets. This
is the final recompense for the desire for paradise:
street after street of tacky shops & borderline lives
hawking some other nation's trinkets. Blare of hi-fi
car stereos & car horns. Terror from anywhere. What
perfect brightness, what peace, we've made with it.
Streets lead to other streets, railroad tracks,
intersections, shimmer of heat & commerce &
a hopelessness that cannot be allowed full expression.
Trains fly down their tracks, clacking, rackety, loud
in their self-regard. In the distance, L.A.'s skyscrapers
await the time-lapse, white clouds. Once the sun re-establishes
its pre-eminence, the city returns to its trades & exchanges,
its sovereign illegalities & illegal remedies. The future, brought
      here, goes
everywhere at once. Bewildered by too much, the city changes,
grows, becomes strange to itself. Highest noon is above,
      unmoving.

Letter to Martin Scorsese

(Casino)

1.

When did flatness become a fabulation of futurity?

2.

Do we still worship the old god of beauty, or have we created a new one, a divinity brutal as the desert, with a garishness as unrelenting as desert light?

3.

Every morning dawn hits the ochre desert with the force of a lost ideal. A wispy lavender rises off the desert floor, gauzy & ethereal, until the sun burns it off, leaving behind the the day's hard edges.

4.

Symmetry calls for harmony and the idea of harmony haunts a highway-edged land, semi-happy in its dissonance.

5.

Was the arterial pulse of neon signs a kind of paradise? Desire lived there, signified by flamingo pink & lime green strips pulsating insistently in the night.

6.

From the sidereal point of view, at night the city is a flat grid, a blackness twinkling with celestial lights. A vast & intense brightness – electric, empyrean.

7.

It dazzled and it blinded, its vast radiance shone clearer than stars.

8.

It was also this: a dark defile, a descent, in which people died needlessly, pointlessly, painfully in the unrestricted emptiness of a sun-struck day.

9.

All the glitz, the glam, the flash, the blam, the book, the vig, the rat, the skim, the take, the heat, the hit, the juice, the mark, the piece, the pinch, the tail, the whack, the wire, the wiseguy, the war the war the war

10.

Measured against the immeasurable universe
no word spoken brought light

From the Notebook of Disappointment
(*Cop Land*)

        story of disappointment, living in plain sight
of the life wanted, pain
of failure as familiar as the pang of desire…

Manhattan skyline at night bejeweled & strung with lights

Every word, an innuendo

Sheer, pathless, the Palisades, "a fence of stakes," rises rock-stiff
    out of the wilderness (still wilderness) above the Hudson

magnificent
        anywhere but here

Brief Chronicle of Desire
(Short Cuts)

From the hills, the city
spreads out against the dawn, an achieved thing

vast against the desert. At night, it's
red, yellow & green dots bright against the darkness.

————

Days repeat themselves again & again
but they're different, as the light is different

from day to day,
sometimes brighter, more brilliant

more declarative, urgent,
rarer.

————

Unspoken losses
that accumulate hour after hour.

————

Waste unheard of, unknown–
epic, & unbelieved.

————

And disconnection:
it hangs in the air with absolute deniability.

———————

Moments in which nothing happens, just
the slow recognition of the strangeness that's overtaking your life.

As in cello arias
drifting onto suburban streets.

———————

Elsewhere, speed & motion: life in a highway-crossed land
means traffic is the new landscape.

———————

The vastness of the city, its sprawl, is
a kind of wish-fulfillment version of happiness, unselfconscious.

———————

Or a new form of ennui,
terrible in its unselfconsciousness.

———————

What do you do when you can't bear
the achievement of your life, your time?

———————

That you can be granted this singular, block-by-block vision of
        the city,

stock-still in the morning light, "bright & glittering in the
    smokeless air,"

arrives like a hope achieved,
like a pain in the heart.

Old-Time Pastoral

(Brother's Keeper)

Old harvesters rusting in
green,
fog-filled fields.

Farms once everywhere, *were*
the land. Now
not even a memory.

In the morning, mist rises,
drifting across old white-washed wooden fences
under a watery, weary-eyed sun.

Then the quiet deepens,
becomes like death,
friendly.

Old Question

(*Goodfellas*)

Dear light of day,

in Astoria, Woodside, Maspeth

at the chrome-wrapped "Airline Diner," at
Sogdiana's & Solemo's

at all the clubs, cafes & delis
in the crowded neighborhoods of the made men,

were you ever embarrassed
at uncovering

the evidence
of our profane

genius?
No, that's

a stupid question.
Spatter-art's our gift, what

we do. Sunlight's
an innocent bystander.

Endlessly – *lovingly* –
we unmake ourselves.

We unmake
ourselves. We

unmake
our

selves.

Art That Shall Ravish

(Full Metal Jacket)

Men without fear   make incalculable beauty.
Through the ruined city   smoke billows out like a phantasm:
it pours out of wall-less structures   roofless temples   shell-
        shocked buildings
drifting out across the river   leaving behind   statues of the living.
Men that move through it know
Fate's angles & trajectories   the paths of least resistance...

From archipelagoes of humiliation come   the need to erase history,
the need   to live unburdened
by the past   by the knowledge
that cracks open dynasties.

When the entire purpose of death is unanswered,
a simple freedom is obtained.   Thought
& action (the dream of a nation) become one.
Pilgrim, ask now for the scribe to write that chronicle,

The one embellished with fabulous ornamentation.
A new empire requires an insular art.
When everything is clean & precise
                                the action
will be beautiful

Variations on a Theme

(Paris, Texas)

All along the highway, strange civilizations congregate in small settlements, like a vision of the past, suddenly there, evident to the eye.

How can a single highway lead to a place in which one mountain is khaki-colored, one sage-green, one lavender, & other ones with improbably deep – improbably light – shades of blue? How can a flat desert highway do this? We were never the land's; the land has never been ours. We're a presumption upon the earth.

A single black ribbon unspools to the horizon's flat line, to a Texas-sized sky. How can it possess such unsullied cumuli – modernist mobiles – exhibiting their casual mastery, their ability to infinitely change, to reinvent themselves in their westward steerage, a performance art beyond any artist.

Cities rise out of the desert. The chrome-clad, cloud-reflecting skyscrapers that huddle in the desert – architectural marvels – can't obscure the fear and loneliness that blows like the wind through city streets, lifting litter here and there.

In the evening, the tall shiny cylinders are lit by a thousand suns, reddest before dying.

A man walks through the desert, surrounded by eroding mesas & terrible loss. The desert is the sum of eons of losses, but the mountains in the distance – belladonna blue – live by a different law. The half-dissolved buttes remember nothing; the man wants to remember nothing.

Paradisiacal light, unsustainable world – the pain of the past, half-forgotten, unsummonable, lives on in the living, we who're left to envy the amnesiac arias of emptiness, here & beyond.

The Wilderness Beckons to the Self
Unknown to the Self
(The Shining)

Wilderness rivering;
mountain-top forests running
to winter's lodge (*Overlook Hotel*) winter-fastened:
snow-drifts drifting to gables.
Spruces crusted in snow.
Outside the vastness is keening; wind-howling, wind-crying.
Whiteness blizzarding, whiting-out roof-pitch & paned-glass
windows.
Past murmuring, past whispering, past halting–
pastness living on in the living,
hush-a-bye-ing,
not knowing,
but trauma-bearing & wearing & worrying
all the while,
scree below snow-capped cliffs & snow-silenced crags.
Overlooking the past, the wilderness
inside: a cold whiteness
pitched past knowing

Message Received

(The Warriors)

                    Something falling

& rising & falling

                    in darkness, pitched past

                    black, the Wonder Wheel

ascends the night sky, the rim

                    of the wheel purple against

                    the nothingness

                    behind it, its spokes

blinking on & off with awful urgency the

                                        cars on the wheel invisible –

mere boxes of yellow dots

                    hanging & rocking back

                    & forth in darkness

where the cars should be –

                    it's all about getting there

doing the thing while you can

                    having the experience before it's too late

                    the words "Wonder Wheel"

seem at first

          a sign of banality

                    commercialism on high

but in actuality

they're beautiful

                    they underestimate

the wheel, the world

                    where laughter should be

                    there's only cold silence

                    distance-distorted, amped beyond

                    the whosh of air, downdraft of desire

On the Land Question

(Days of Heaven)

The way afternoon sunlight fills the land with light
      is the way
the mind tries to take in the fact of beauty. The wind
      ruffles the back of wheat fields,
a waving expanse of gold moving in unison,
      swaying back & forth to the horizon.
The landscape's limitless – shimmering – lives in constant
      motion, responsive to its own ends. It's hard
to take in the unanimity of such luminosity.
      There's a radiance to the vastness, a sense of secret lives,
a shine to the world above the loam.
      It's 1916, it's 1978: labor versus capital again,
harvesting & profiting from the harvesting,
      the tale of people who've only themselves to sell,
the old story of sectioning
      a life into days, short-term loss reckoned
against the ledger hope of long-term gain.
      Over & above the gentle undulations, a soft light plays out:
it's late afternoon, in the permanent evening of August's end:
      who gets to see the land as beautiful?
The sun never whitens, never lessens its labors in luminosity,
      never delivers less than
a dazzling optics of the land ripening at its richest hour.

For Maribel Foley

The Emigrants Go West, Go West, Go West
(*Stroszek*)

Dusk a pink-&-vermillion-gashed sky –
   the big-screen beauty of it says, learn to die
      & afterwards cars with their headlights on race
        into darkness until
          the flatness of the land swallows them
            never touching what it is they came for...

Shares

(Harlan County, USA)

In the long descent, / darkness / the one true compass. The world is not one; there are worlds within worlds / what we know of the world of light is less than the weight of a soul slipping from an earth-pressed body. We have lost many a word / lost many a word / & for them they go / down / rock is sky overhead / in the darkness a ray of light / in the darkness there's clarity / you can see / the children of children / "the immense possibilities of breath." / In the darkness / you can feel the lamentation in the / air / can see the gift of blood / the remoteness of heaven. / And of the market / its shares, / the world is silent. The words the words / in the darkness / everything turns on the words: / "my people"

American Dialogue

(Taxi Driver)

The days go on & on.
Night goes on & on.

Red neon signs
shimmer on wet streets.

Loneliness like a traffic light
blinking in the night.

Reflections in plate-glass windows of
people no longer there.

And one other thing:

your face with someone else's eyes
in the mirror –

Who is talking to whom?

The Unregenerate Who Once
Wanted to Be Redeemed
(Chinatown)

A film about a town by Robert Towne. A film about a town within a town, Chinatown. A film partially about a Los Angeles scandal in the early part of the 20th century (the story of the nefarious 1908 Owens Valley "Rape" and scandalous San Fernando Valley land-grab by speculators). A film about Jack Nicholson. A film about Hollis Mulwray, a character derived from LA's real-life water engineer William Mullholland (the general manager of LA's Bureau of Water Works & Supply) – the name of the character Hollis Mulwray a clever anagram for "Mullholland." A film about – of course – Los Angeles in the '30s, a city of broad avenues, palm trees, green watered lawns & silent mansions serviced by silent Chinese staff. A film about power, rape & incest: about the courtliness of true decadence. A film about the past never being past, about the way the present is just part of the revolution of the wheel of history, something we only gradually come to perceive. A film about the sadness of discovering that American democracy is a façade. A film about a Mexican boy who comes out of the dusk riding a palomino on a dried-up river-bed delivering cryptic messages. A film about children who are lost & never find their way back. A noir film about other noir films, about moonless darkness & the daytime dazzle of Los Angeles streets. A film about Venetian blinds & blind desire. A film about abandoned box springs, broken cabinets and furniture detritus, their brokenness somehow lovely next to the mountains in the morning desert light. A film about never regretting what you do; a film about always regretting what you do. A film about what you can never do. A film about being lost between the desert & the sea.

White Days, Interruption

(One Flew Over the Cuckoo's Nest)

                    The horizon of all possibilities
returns as the muffled terror of institutions –
gleaming waxed floors
long corridors & locked rooms
stretch into interminable futures

wherein whiteness is the administration of days
which
will not suffer a whit of deviation
or allow more than a rectangle of sky –

The wind blows in squalls
and between clouds & clouds
words shrivel the will

but if one were to say that words   could be prayers
if one were to say that words could be love   or tokens of love
if one were to say that words could grieve

then the wind that blows in squalls might be the sound of elegies
through the pines
                    & the fog at dusk could be said to be settling back
on the green forests & the black mountains,
                                        hushed & hushing
a syllabic quietness
demanding nothing
vanishing at dawn

From Brooklyn Bridge
(*The French Connection*)

Even given decaying brownstones & iron fire-escapes,
    the tragedy of "the White Lady"
no longer seems so tragic,
              & what
    then does that say
          about our sense of "the tragic?"

At the water's edge, the neo-Gothic
          towers of the Brooklyn Bridge
proportion the air,
      the twinned cathedral-window spaces
  frame the ideal of possibility, even
beauty. Brooklyn

may be a borough of bodegas,
          luncheonettes, etc.,
for this or that individual, but
in linking itself to that other world of
          "The City,"
the bridge makes possible
  a two-way trafficking that calls into question
    the singularity of the distinction.

It's a question of twinness. Justice
  too. For when
      has it been unalloyed
pure, unadulterated? If listened to,

it has a tell, intentions
beyond the intentions; it gives
itself
away.

Poem Reflecting on How the West Was Won
(The Missouri Breaks)

just seeing   at a great distance
the "fine high country of Montana"   the ravines
gulches & grassy plains with the dandelions

                    waving in the breeze
is enough; no denying it – there's grandeur –
    inexpressible mountain ranges – inexpressible high country air –
    but what
            is enough? The great horizontality of place
refuses fine measurements

                    greenness has spead, is spreading
midst waste & ruin –
            the blackened frame of a burnt-out cabin is
            situated in it –
at a great distance   anything can be forgiven, forgotten –
    how the big country swallows up everything
    big & small
            as if the only history was now   dandelion seeds taking to
    the air   the Missouri getting flashier
the faster its currents go

                    sun-spangles on the water

"What shall I say? I was seized by a distemper..."

Time Lapse

(Grey Gardens)

Whether you can tell from this distance   what
the house was before it was
consumed by wildness, by rampant

greenery is only partly the point. Its grand dreams have aged,
the ravage, evident to the eye.

Devoured by whispers   what remains
remains grey-shingled & silver shadowed.

Green leaves whisper ruin, vines whisper ruin; boughs whisper
        ruin...

Whispers of things not allowed. Of things someone
thought was said.

The present's the movie of the past, a dialogue of disembodied
        voices,
each talking to the other, over the other, a polyphonic
        contestation of desire
undiminished by time.

The rooms   the lonely rooms   echo with them.

The ocean – a thin ribbon of blue – contends in its own element
with a never-ending susurration.

From the outside, you can barely see the faces through the
        window screens.

From the interior – the dim, decrepit interior – the long windows
        are full of leaves & light.

Scarecrow

(Scarecrow)

desert highway   long line
of telephone poles

climbing to a mountain range – what
mountains are these? They're

lovely & low   barren & laid-back
with a blackness

like that of   the sky
But why

is
the sky purple-black?

Why is the one lone hill crowned
by an oak tree, fully-spread?

Why bound by barbed-wire?
Why fence a tree like that,

a hill like that?
It's openness we want,

wanting to be
elsewhere,

endless openness,
endlessly beckoning,

with no goodbyes,
nothing indecipherable.

Letter to Terrence Malick
(*Badlands*)

Coming to an end   with no expectation of fulfillment
the world is stunning
in its slowness. Weeks
& weeks of waving fields & empty skies.
Rivers that bend
round serpentine banks & cottonwood groves.
The great blood-orange sun that finally sets
extinguishes the last, fond hopes.
The vastness of the sky guarantees
a new imperium, a loneliness
that will be epic,
but felt in the heart, like an old pain.
Strange devices that once recorded voices
whisper past their passing.
On the great plains
on its wind-swept, wide-open spaces,
the whispering rises,
static hiss of old vinyl,
no more no more,
everything as it was.

Not Even a Dream

(*Deliverance*)

Riverwater rushes downstream   whitewater over blackrock, over
ragged rockcleft   past lean-to, boulder-slabs on the riverbank –
frenzy of fast water meeting riverrock,
the force of it   a cry in the heart   carrying itself beyond
the echoes of other cries   echoes fainter in the churning.
Part of the green, fog-shrouded, humid wilderness,
part of the night sky – a full moon cloud-ringed in darkness –

                                                                the river
wholly takes itself as itself, insensate to suffering.

Flowing past the rusted-out car-hulls sinking into river banks,
the little white clapboard church &
the grave-yard being emptied of its graves   the river
is deathlessly complete
passionless in its turbulence   so flat in its final afterfalls serenity
the trees half down in it

Speed of Desire

(Bullitt)

Speed, arc of highway, sweetness
of the ephemeral:

> the – city – the hills, the streetcars – the bay as
> backdrop. A blurring: simplification
> of "the most fundamental questions…"

The thrill of chasing death, the heroism of
the single individual
who would defeat X & restore
Y…
Against that, the sheer
thrill of speed: eros of law & lawlessness.
The fable–the fabled hills of the fabled city –
excites
a purely propulsive desire. The city

falls away; the hills & streetcars, the white structures, the blue
expanse of the bay,
disappears
behind a curved glare of glass.
The thrill of seeming
to go past everything.

The thrill of never having to look back   of never having to leave
the car.

To Feel the Wholeness of the World
(Cool Hand Luke)

The sun writes in his Book, a sentence of
heat & light heat & light.

Righteousness in the scald of days.

The grass is singing, to the sling blades swinging, the grass is singing.

To feel the wholeness of the world about you: that's the only thing.

The only thing, Boss, I just want to move over here move over here.

Here there is no other.

There is among us no element that is not lawless

not the sun, not the men working under the sun, nor the men
watching the men who are working under the sun

dying to be free.

Black single-lane highways cut through a God-stricken land like a
bereavement.

Something shimmering in the heat of a late summer day.

Fields goldsoftened by light.

In the sweat-box, dark hand-me-down minutes.

Somewhere: wind whispering through trees. A black-ribboned
coolness. Moonlight.

Goodbye to All That
(*Point Blank*)

Islanded hope, rusted steel;
Over the water, a beautiful city rises up

> *desire like the dream of paradise*

The Golden Gate Bridge, weightless & elegant,
soars above suspended lives

> *desire like the dream of paradise*

What you *were* under bright neon light,
walking over the sheen of waxed floors

> *desire like the dream of paradise*

Morning light: corporate, mercenary
intent upon the business of business

> *desire like the dream of paradise*

Bric-a-brac of the everyday,
lives traded for it

> *desire like the dream of paradise*

At night, sharp shadows;
broken breaths & betrayal

> *desire like the dream of paradise*

Emptiness of Alcatraz,
its cavernous concord & silence

desire like the dream of paradise

Repose, Desire, Darkness
(Bonnie and Clyde)

Stillness. Summer heat.
The call of languor & of death.
The Texas sky was high & hot & blue
untouched –
the quietness
explosive.
The blue won't talk about it.
Was it late or early
the time when there was a hill –
high grass waving in the sun –
nothing on it,
no trees or roads
when they streaked down it,
tore across it. A running away
that was a running toward.
Great wheat-colored dust clouds
wheeling behind them like an afterthought,
nerve-endings fever-pitched with foreboding.
Omens all along the way, easy to read.
Just wanting
the still repose of the field
on a summer day,
its openness & space.
The claim it could make on other days.

Bad

(The Good, the Bad, the Ugly)

Ruin's a dangerous thing,
        stove-in hovels & filth, mangy-ness in man & beast–
a romanticism like the bare foothills in the distance,
                        the big bowl of sky above

not quite cloudless & blue…

A New Chorus

(The Birds)

The earth   open to the sky
receives a graceful light.   The ocean shimmers
along the high California cliffs –
in the openness of the American century
the light falls everywhere –
the clean, well-ordered streets,
the curving Pacific highway,
the white cluster of a village nestled
against the bay.

At the edges,
          forces
                that cannot be acknowledged
flock together, gather strength
for a final assault.

People
      schooled
in unremembered pain, observe
in silence the
          portents
                shaping themselves
         in a blank sky.

Here strange mansions ring out with rote singing
& the dead bleed from empty eye-sockets.
But the true horror is the horror of the perfect coiffure.

The world as we wanted it to be signaling
no more. Bird cries & wingflaps

louder than desire. A new chorus
sounds, rising over the land.

Thinking outside of thought.
Water's edge darkens in elegy.
The world to us:
I will dream you.

Southlandia

(Cape Fear)

Pure fact of the world   wilderness as wilderness was.
Black currents ripple blackly.   Upriver
river banks press close   broad-based cypresses
draped
with Spanish moss look spectral   ghosts from another age next
to   old-growth oak & pine. Stillness
as thick as green vines   a scene
of green vegetation run riot   a wildness
in the land   less land than waterland
strange hybrid of solidity & fluidity   nothing conquered
nothing contained   the visible merely
one aspect   of a world vanishing upon sight.
And when there's an opening   it comes as a relief
a place where sunlight doesn't die   but lingers on the water
the green pushed back for a while.   Named & renamed, the
river
survives in the violence of its going.   Did we take wildness as
          our book,
its tangled calligraphy as script?   Of all the lessons why
that one?   Glossy-surfaced, black, the river cannot but
mirror the trees & ferns   the green world around it.

Synesthesia of the Artificial
(*Rio Bravo*)

"pulling away from all the hardened fakery, the camera lingers on a free-standing Saguaro outside a made-to-order Western town, its thick limbs silhouetted against a night sky, patient in its distance from the astral world. In its solitariness, it evokes a 1950s sense of time & space. You can see it as an image of stoic self-sufficiency, even endurance, in the face of the indignities of the age; equally, you can see it as an image of pathos, the outstretched limbs of the cactus appearing to implore the star-speckled heavens (for what the film does not say)..."

Infatuation

(North by Northwest)

It's not the ephemerality of things, but their crowded everydayness, as charged as a brief infatuation: America at mid-century filled with shimmering skyscrapers, sleek silvery trains & cocktail confidence – sheer joy with the merest tinge of paranoia; error & doubt just beneath the surface. Everyone playing a part – the right man, the wrong man: what matters is what you are thought to be

It's not the gridwork of graph paper, but a frenetic intersection of geometric lines that one day becomes a New York city skyscraper, the chimera of the glass surface reflecting a fun-house version of rush hour in which midtown Manhattan's warped yellow taxis drive straight through the borders of the real: after all, nothing's impossible, anything can become anything, the kinetic momentum of a decade takes us clear into a new place, a new self-love, charmed & charming

"It's not what happens to Cary Grant; it's about what happens to his suit," the grey flannel suit of the Madison Avenue ad man, Roger O Thornhill, the "O" which is said to stand for nothing by the man who said "There is no such thing as a lie. There's only expedient exaggeration." The medium grey Glen check single-breasted suit by Kilgour French & Stanbury, through kidnapping, murder & attempted murder, does not crumple or crease. O Roger Roger Roger

It's not just a plane in the sky; it's death coming out of the blue, a bi-plane crop-duster come on a mission, come to do harm on a day in which the flatness of the plain makes the crossroads below look country-sad, country-small. See the solitary play of the plane as it tilts its wings & turns into the emptiness of the sky, its buzzing drone as it swoops down; against the vastness of the plains & the sky, observe its single-minded refusal to be distracted by the world, the elegance of the man running

Fictions of the Ones You Love
(*Vertigo*)

Not the life   dreamt of
but the one found while living it –
terrors & fears,
the past plunging down   like a bottomless nightmare –

it's all real.
The troubling dreams, the troubling fictions are real.
The fictions of the ones you love are real –
like a painting whose artifice outshines
the subject of the painting.

The white domed church overlooking the blue bay,
the cemetery obelisks next to the thin, blood-orange gladiolas,
& the mysterious woman fading   into a forest dusk

are radiant with strange meanings.
Haze of desire over
every object of desire:

fear of paradise,
fear from panic.

The tragedy of never ever knowing.

Borderlands

(Touch of Evil)

"as the camera moves

through the streets of the Mexican border town
the plan was to feature
a succession of different and contrasting
Latin American musical numbers –
the effect, that is, of
our passing one cabaret orchestra after another. In

honky-tonk districts on the border,
loudspeakers are over
the entrance of every joint, large or small,
each blasting out its own tune
by way of a "come on" or "pitch"

for the tourists. The fact that the streets are
invariably loud with this music

was planned as a basic device
throughout the entire picture. The
special use of contrasting mambo-type rhythm numbers

with rock'n'roll

should be developed... also
either the shot itself,
or its placing,

should have
a bewildering effect:
one just doesn't know
what's happening..."

Vistavision Feeling

(The Searchers)

Nothing we love   is what we love –
not strange then that this land could be
so loved.   Inside a darkened theater   vintage VistaVision clouds
pile up against a VistaVision sky.
The ochre-red desert shades into distances purply-blue.

What is this world but a world of left-overs,
the desert the mesas the high self-regarding buttes
                              the wildflower & sagebrush
testaments to worlds gone by –
                    rock-time ledgered in the rock-face.
The searchers ride past it   furious for what isn't there.

Men in war paint know this & must die.
Do bleed sweetly onto the desert floor.
Do savagely demise.
With all the strong, short-timers thundering by.

Postcards to Hitchcock

(*The Wrong Man*)

Guilt/ secrets of the heart/ fallen hopes. Shadows of cell-block bars faint on the faces of the innocent.

———

Shadowy mis-en-scène of New York in the fifties – dark narrow streets, big rounded cars, thick brick walls. You always gave us images of ourselves watching others, watching movies, watching the world. For entertainment, we watch ourselves watching ourselves.

———

Some might say that watching the routine machinations of authority abusing authority is a metaphor for the protocols of the authoritarian state in which bit-by-bit, regulation-by-regulation, human dignity is methodically stripped away, leaving people who are alive but dead. All of us, traces of what might have been...

———

Some have said that the film is nothing but clichés, evidence of an imagination that has exhausted itself upon noir-ish plots. I think, though, that clichés, are like monuments to heroic moments or individuals, unseen but not quite forgotten, weakly bearing the energetic force of another time.

———

Is the happy ending eye-candy for the masses? Or did you do it to dramatize its sweetness, its artificiality?

———

More and more now say that the masses don't exist, that it is, and always was, a made-up thing, as unreal as, say, a wingéd horse. Some say there are only individuals, as distinct from one another as a horse is from a wingéd horse.

——

Some say that the film lacks suspense, is unwatchable. I think that it is unwatchable because it's so terrifying.

——

There's so much terror now, Hitch. It's there, or in the background, like the noise from the street. Can that be normal? Perhaps what makes terror terror is its novelized normalcy, a half-real, half-unreal feeling, a story that both wants & fears its ending.

——

Fear too – what is it but the price of knowledge?

——

Some say the only proof against power is beauty; the only proof of the world is beauty.

——

O fable-maker, all I can see is that pain's the progenitor of beauty, proof of nothing requiring proof...

Spencer Tracy's Silver Train Transverses the Desert of Death Valley with Jagged Mountains in the Distance

(Bad Day at Black Rock)

    "such a

          heartless

                      immensity"

Hurt

(Singing in the Rain)

The steps   the graceful, self-regarding
steps   the

        leaps

the whirling   balletic
leaps
                for a moment
pure promise
                finds
an exultant heart.

How to describe
the nonchalant fluidity of that body –

everything we might be, entrusted
to grace
                    the heart's full song...

Insouciance of the umbrella flipping
in midair (death
                be gone, fear be gone, lovelessness
be gone...)

were we ever that beautiful?

Or Maybe It Was Hollywood
(Sunset Boulevard)

Time turned a mansion into a cracked-marble ruin.
Time turned recollection into reportage.
Time turned bluster into blackmail.
Time turned innocence into injury.
Time turned silence into speech (then back to silence again).
Time turned sunlight streaming into sunlight leaving.
Time turned bygones into broken mirrors.
Time turned the asylum of theater into theatricality.
Time turned fealty into forgery.
Time turned guests into goldfinches.
Time turned greatness into glimmers of day.
Time turned a narcissus bouquet into naked rain.
Time turned a ghost whispering "You?" into

                                    you, you, you.

Letter to John Huston
(*Key Largo*)

                                        innocence of the Atlantic
sparkling
in the open air. Palm trees bend down
whispering secrets of old sins.   The shoreline halts
before bright sunlight   skittering free across sateened water.
What's most free is most destructive   the becalmed water rises up
in a fury of wind   white waves roll back into black water
the key a thin strand of sand is   battered again & again
as if in revenge for all the insults.   O hooded-eyed romancer,
the insults have only gotten worse.   Nature
is out of joint   & fix-it-all heroism
is a fondness   from a silver-screened world.
The earth wants us gone.

Western Fable

(Yellow Sky)

How the entire story must be in black & white, a story of stark
opposites.
Six figures dazed on a dazzling-white salt-flat:
above them, darkness fills the sky, Western-epic style.

Beyond the scalloped whiteness, mountains
rise up, are elemental, a massed black solidity.
The story is the story of slashing forces with tiny mounted
figures,

black mounted fables, little more than shadows, mirage-
stepping across a
shimmering desert,
inscapes metaphoric & metamorphic, inconstant as the sea.

White glitter, flight, convergence under a dying sun.
To turn a life into value: to not
die a flickering shadow: that

one desire is what makes the land endlessly large, endlessly
lonely.
The hunt: to be storied, to enter someone's story, to be named
in the mind.
To be transformed. To be another self in the making.

To be *of* not *in.*
To leave *taking* & partake of *doing.*
To finally give up counting as bad faith.

To walk out the door
& see ruin everywhere,
& not see anything like tragedy

Cities Like We Thought They'd Be
(Dead Reckoning)

How everything is far away
and long deceased   that world of plain
hotel rooms with squat black phones
radiating menace
is gone   but
other frailties persist
what we know
turns out to be different from what
we thought we knew   people
we think we know   have secret
pasts   different identities
& the whole tangled plot of their lives
can be disentangled
without really getting to the bottom of it
in 1940s noir
it's the sheer physicality of the social world
that's on display
ordinary objects
elevated to the epochal –
the open phonebook
as lethal as a revolver –
cities eerie
in the way they resemble cities –
fever dreams
of light & darkness
blinking faster & faster
like the return of buried memories
the silver screen
nostalgic for a deceased world
before it's even deceased

B-Movie Drama

(The Dark Corner)

Odd to watch an old *film noir*
on a bright winter day
by oneself
in an empty house.
It feels voyeuristic
observing
a distant decade's mannered
feelings,
the compositional tension of
darkness & shadows
on city streets (chiaroscuro
of Broadway's
lightbulb marquees) –
the darkness & dread lit up,
something
antique but familiar,
like the afterwash of a nightmare.
Odd the way sunlight
filters through curtains
trying to bleach out
the old darkness,
trying to lighten
the screen's
obdurate blackness.
It's the set-up,
& the struggle
against the set-up,
that commands
attention: the
character

as much as
the actor. You
watch them struggle.
But who remembers
the characters or
the actors –
much less the fear –
as they find the fate
that's been awaiting them
all their lives.

Letter to John Ford

(*Grapes of Wrath*)

                          then the road could be
something other than a path of flight,
an escape from the all-pervasive
powers of iniquity…

The largeness of the land's a gesture in itself,
                        a vastness that in evening
or early morning unveils
               a momentary luminosity, when darkness
is forestalled
or limned against
                    light's gathering effulgence,
revealing the desert's stark theater.

Silence in the surround of it.

      Like a plea it murmurs,
      less light less light less light

Landscape with Emotion
(*The Wizard of Oz*)

We have lost the way & do not know how to get back.
The sky is dark, darkening, black & blackening, poised
like a curse over the land

a-whipping, a-disheveling a-disordering
the unpaved road runs flat to the horizon, everything warped
& weathered

a land stripped down, sepia-brown, seen at once
as it is and as it was, a hard land
with leafless trees

& wind-blown fences, gale-force winds rending ripping & roaring,
the blistered clapboards screeching, the fierceness of the desire to
make this dirt-blown patch
home

the desire to find in the world's uncontained ferocity an
                incommensurate
love stronger than the gale-winds that rage round the child
                the child
looking for anything like home

The Landscape That Makes Language Less Than Any Rustling in the Wind

(Stagecoach)

Nowhere does anything ask anything of you –
the high buttes, mesas & spires
that rise from the impossibly ochre desert floor
are monuments
to light, eons
burnt into stone;
time striated into rock.
A grand concord of elementality
has long since taken dominion.
Space here is wider,
older than desire.
The sky –
a vaulted, cloudless blue –
provides the inexpressible theatrics.
But say you wanted to say
"beauty." Say
you wanted to say
"landscape" or even "stunning."
In the concord of indifference
beyond indifference
that marks the land,
syllables would linger
in the crystalline air.
After that, a waiting-out
that makes language
cryptic, then less than any
rustling in the wind.

Cinematography of the Soul
(City Lights)

Amidst the suffering   there's the question
of who really sees whom
what really goes on is   invisible –
rose petals in the gutter –
the monumentality of Los Angeles in the 'twenties –
black shadows on white marble –
defines
the era   the century
I'm thinking too of
the black luster of the millionaire's limo
of starkness versus pathos
the cinematography of the soul
which vexes the viewer
who wants something   who
watches someone who has given
everything
to be scorned   the tramp
who does the unthinkable
without thought
dares the viewer
the era   the century
then on city streets
a little light
a little gift
an ordinary afternoon
& the world stunned
into silence –
speechless before speechlessness–

Memory Fragment: New York
in Black & White Circa the 1920s
(*The Crowd*)

& then
as in a fever Manhattan
filled a sky with skyscrapers

from the water
the black skyline appeared huge & deathless,
shrouded in fog

Letter to Chaplin

(The Kid)

Remembering you, I'm remembering us – or your imagined, hoped-for version of us. I'm remembering the Tramp who could not help but find himself in the shabbiness of run-down Olvera Street. Shambling, or as the occasion demanded, running in your trademark herky-jerky way from the law. Who struggled against hard-heartedness & casual cruelty, holding fast onto the child who – can it be said otherwise? – stole his heart. I'm remembering, too, a director who screened a language "of eyes and smiles, of eyes and affection." Would that there could be homage to that. Would that there could be homage to the wordless warmth – the wit – of your films, but words can't match the power of faces *seeing* one another, fully seeing one another. The language of eyes has always been greater than that of tongues. But, as it turns out, it does *help*, at least, to cry out – to address the ones you love, even as they're being separated from you. I think of your films as comic (tragic) statements against all the powers that would separate us from happiness. Pathos in the recognition that we've created those powers– systems & institutions – that dominate and disfigure us. Though often regarded as fearful, it's the fierceness of The Tramp that strikes me. His willingness to honor what one should not be ashamed to identify the heart's desire. Of all the faces in film, only his is at once hopeful, knowing, wry, tender & sad. It gives the screen an extraordinary intensity, an extraordinary intimacy. A felt sense of possibility, that the world can be remade, that injustice, poverty & despair can be redeemed. A felt sense that it can vanquish small-mindedness and tightly-sealed ideals. Sorry that we became what we did. Did the Tramp, also, despair of us? Can he *simply* despair? Deepest regrets for our mean-minded, petty failures. For using too many words.

Sunday Afternoon Thing
(Birth of a Nation)

Ceaseless this   wandering epic.
Flickering black-and-white figures   frame
the collective fever dream.   The smoke
that clears from barren hills &   burning towns

is the pastoral   laid to waste.

What is the smoke that billows across the screen
but the beginning of "the modern spectacle"? The beginning
of "the ascendancy of the image" over
                       human suffering?

Innocence like a darkening sky,
like a city in ruin, like
the avid edge of a blade...

                   O what do we want to *be*?

All the bodies holding   clasping,   embracing
other bodies –

with the dead on the ground no longer whispering names.

"So much ash to be blessed."

Notes

"You Think It's You But It's Really Not" appropriates words and phrases from Tim Smith-Laing's translation of Paul Valéry's "The Cemetery by the Sea," published in Issue 5 of *Wave Composition*: http://www.wavecomposition.com/article/issue-5/the-cemetery-by-the-sea/

"Letter to Martin Scorsese": The final lines of the poem are from Frank Bidart's "The Old Man at the Wheel," in *Watching the Spring Festival*

In "Shares," "the immense possibilities of breath" is from Peter Riley's *Excavations*.

"Borderlands": The poem's language has been fashioned out of Orson Welles' lengthy December 5, 1957 memo to Universal Studios. The preview version that Orson Welles saw of his film occasioned a 50-page passionate objection to the studio's butchered version of it.

"Spencer Tracy's Silver Train Transverses the Desert of Death Valley with Jagged Mountains in the Distance" quotes from Herman Melville's *Moby Dick*.

"Letter to Chaplin": "of eyes and smiles, of eyes and affection" is lifted from Peter Gizzi's "Vincent, Homesick for the Land of Pictures" in *The Outernationale*.

"Sunday Afternoon Thing" contains a line from Paul Celan.

Acknowledgements

I'd like to thank editors of the following journals for publishing the following poems, sometimes with different titles:

491 Magazine: "Infatuation"
1913: A Journal of Forms: "Cities Like We Thought They'd Be," "Cinematography of the Soul," "Art That Shall Ravish"
American Literary Review: "You Think It's You, But It's Really Not"
Colorado Review: "Sunday Afternoon Thing"
The Common: "Snow as Different Versions of Things," "Borderlands"
Hayden's Ferry Review: "Letter to Martin Scorsese," "Postcards to Hitchcock"
Jacket 2: "Fictions of the One You Love," "Not Even a Dream," "Time Lapse," "White Days" (forthcoming)
Jerry Magazine: "Panic That Dares Not Speak Its Own Name"; "Landscape with Emotion," "Letter to John Huston"
Map Literary: "Shares"
Mayday: "Letter to Charlie Chaplin"
Molly Bloom: "Brief Chronicle of Desire," "From the Notebook of Disappointment," "On the Land Question," "The Wilderness Beckons to the Self Unknown to the Self," "Poem Reflecting on How the West Was Won," "Spencer Tracy's Silver Train Transverses the Desert of Death Valley with Jagged Mountains in the Distance"
Quiddity: "Landscape That Makes Language Less and Less," "Letter to John Ford"
Shearsman magazine: "The Emigrants Go West, Go West, Go West," "A New Chorus"
The White Review: "Letter to Jim Jarmusch"
Witness (online): "The Unregenerate Who Once Wanted to Be Redeemed," "To Feel the Wholeness of the World"
Zone Magazine: "Southlandia"

I'd also like to thank Jennifer Atkinson, Suzanne Chester, Matthew Cooperman, Tony Frazer, Peter Gizzi, Nick Halpern, Antony Harrison, Brenda Hillman, Christopher Kondrich, Thomas Lisk, Leila May, Elaine Orr, Eric Pankey, Ethel Rackin, Sharon Setzer, Susan Stewart and Chris Tonelli for their interest in, and support of, this book.

Lightning Source UK Ltd.
Milton Keynes UK
UKHW042110120419
340943UK00001B/8/P